# THE

# CLIENT'S GUIDE

# — TO —

## CAR ACCIDENT & INJURY CASES

### THE INFORMATION THE INSURANCE COMPANIES DON'T WANT YOU TO HAVE

**ML** LAW OFFICES | **Mike Lombardi** & **ASSOCIATES**

**INJURY AND ACCIDENT LAWYERS**

1011 SMITH STREET

PROVIDENCE, RI 02908

PHONE: 401 751 6100

EMAIL: ML@LOMBARDIRUSSO.COM

WEBSITE: WWW.LOMBARDILAWOFFICE.COM

ISBN: 978-1-63385-181-8

*Designed and published by*

Word Association Publishers
205 Fifth Avenue
Tarentum, Pennsylvania 15084

www.wordassociation.com
1.800.827.7903

# TABLE OF CONTENTS

# PREFACE

MICHAEL LOMBARDI, OF MIKE LOMBARDI & ASSOCIATES – Injury and Accident Lawyers , has been helping accident and injury victims his entire career. He's been a staple in the southern New England personal injury area of the law.

Michael's main concentration includes all areas of personal injury law and criminal defense. He's helped thousands of people and families throughout Rhode Island and Massachusetts with personal injury, auto accident, and criminal defense cases.

He attended Rhode Island College in Providence, where he graduated in 2001 with a bachelor of science in political science. He attended Roger Williams School of Law and earned a juris doctorate in 2005.

He has many professional affiliations including the Rhode Island Bar Association, Member of the Massachusetts Bar, American Bar Association, Member of United States District Court, District of Rhode Island, and Justinian Law Society.

Michael is licensed to practice law in the federal and state courts of Rhode Island and Massachusetts, and he has extensive experience in civil and criminal litigation and all aspects of personal injury claims with an impressive record of success.

# INTRODUCTION

I'VE WRITTEN THIS BOOK SPECIFICALLY TO HELP THOSE who have been victims of personal injury and their families overcome the devastating impact that such injuries can wreak on their lives not only in the short term but also in the future.

It may not be possible to make victims of personal injuries completely "whole" again, but this book will answer many of their questions and ideally point a way out of the devastation—financial, emotional, and social—that such accidents can cause.

My experience has taught me that personal injuries can have long-lasting as well as short-term ramifications for victims and their families. My experience has also taught me that those ramifications can be eased by thoughtful, thorough legal help that results in a just settlement or award. Such an award or settlement can cover that initial ambulance ride, the emergency room care, and lost wages as well as costs on a longer horizon, such as rehabilitation or needed surgery that becomes necessary even years after an accident.

> Personal injuries can have long-lasting as well as short-term ramifications for victims and their families.

On top of the "tangible" costs and losses, victims of personal injury can claim future wages they will lose out on, pain and suffering, and the physical therapy and psychological counseling some victims sometimes require to get their lives back on an even keel.

Let's consider the matter in these terms: a personal injury can cause a loss of dignity—economic, social, familial, and personal—that a just settlement can help restore. This can come about through mediation with insurance companies, settlement that requires mediation, or even going to trial. One way or another, our law firm will strive to help you get back on your feet and receive a settlement or award that will compensate you for all the damages you have suffered.

We've helped a good number of clients over the years obtain the justice they deserved. Also, we take pride in knowing that those who were responsible for the accidents were put on notice that their workplace conditions, driving habits, behaviors, equipment or tools they design and sell—you name it—are dangerous. We're sure our work on behalf of our clients has had the effect of stopping others from having to suffer due to other parties' negligence, willful ignorance, or lack of concern. It's not far-fetched to say that our efforts in pursuing justice for our clients may have stopped others from suffering catastrophic injuries, even death.

We specialize in personal injury, and we put the accent on "personal,"—not corporate, institutional, or governmental injury. Our clients are injured folks whose agony is compounded by the suffering their families are going through, all the time wondering if they will ever get the justice they deserve.

Personal injury cases very frequently call for a rapid and complete investigation of the scene of an automobile accident, a "slip-and-fall," a piece of machinery, and so on. Should someone have cleaned up a spill? Was the other driver drunk? Did a power tool have adequate warning labels?

We'll solicit expert advice from engineers or investigators in different fields, and we'll interview and get statements from witnesses before they move or their memories fade. We'll work to make sure the tool, the appliance, the car—whatever—is not thrown away, sold, or junked. We'll look into whether training programs and safety regulations existed and were followed and determine if they were inadequate for the risks involved.

We also look to uncover all the parties who shared responsibility and blame for these accidents, because frequently there can be two, three, or even more parties whose actions contributed to an accident.

In addition, we will exert a great deal of effort into determining future lost wages as well as the long-term medical, emotional, and social needs of victims of personal injury. We know from experience that such injuries can have not only long-lasting affects but also can cause problems that may not show up for years. Today's broken leg may result in the need for a knee replacement twenty years from now; smoke from a fire that damaged lungs could result in the need for respiratory care in a decade. Though a great deal of time can separate cause and effect, victims of personal injury deserve to know such possible long-term outcomes.

> Today's broken leg may result in the need for a knee replacement twenty years from now.

We all know that certain injuries—say a broken wrist or even a bad cut—will heal, and life will move on, but other injuries—a broken back or a serious burn, for instance—can leave someone with permanent physical disabilities and disfigurements whose effects could last forever.

It's for these reasons that we focus not only on the short-term problems our clients face but also on making them aware of the long-term needs that may arise in their cases. Our efforts are aimed at getting them the compensation they deserve as well as the justice they're due.

This book cannot answer all your questions. My years of experience with personal injury cases have taught me that each case is unique, and every victim of personal injury is an individual. That said, it's my hope that this short book will give you an idea of the range of questions that have to be asked and answered, the details that needs to be gathered, and most important, the rights that victims of personal injury deserve to be respected.

> Each case is unique, and every victim of personal injury is an individual.

This book is not to be taken as legal advice; no book can take the place of a competent personal injury attorney looking over all the facts of your case, coming up with questions you may not have thought about, and digging into the details. It's only at that point that you and I can come up with the best way of proceeding.

My law firm has earned the respect of the courts, the insurance companies we frequently do battle with, and, much more important, the many clients I've served. The respect my firm has is due to the success I've consistently demonstrated in personal injury cases through the resources and the dedication I bring to bear on each case I accept.

Those on our staff have the sensitivity, compassion, and knowledge victims of personal injury can rely on to make a difficult and confusing situation—with implications for today and tomorrow—less traumatic.

# 1

# YOUR PERSONAL INJURY/AUTO ACCIDENT

PERSONAL INJURIES CAN BE THE RESULT OF MEDICAL malpractice, assault and battery, an automobile accident, a faulty tool or appliance, someone's failure to take necessary steps to prevent an accident, a dog bite—the list is endless. They can be the result of another party's negligence, a willful act, or even a failure to act. Survivors of someone killed intentionally or due to another party's negligence can suffer personal injury for that death and can make "wrongful death" claims.

Our experience in dealing with personal injury cases has taught us that these accidents can happen in so many different ways and for so many different reasons. We've been schooled in those many ways, and we know the incredible importance of getting the right expert investigators, forensic experts, engineers, and other scientists who have the experience and expertise to investigate an auto accident site, a defective product, or a store that didn't keep spills mopped up. Their work can go a long way toward determining the cause: faulty installation, bad design, lack of maintenance—you name it, we've found it.

Unfortunately, personal injury victims are not always able to do the research and investigation necessary to determine if any of these errors caused or contributed to an accident. However, we've had experience in setting the wheels of a thorough investigation in motion to determine the cause or causes of an accident and any elements (lack of safety measures, faulty maintenance, lack of warnings) that could have contributed to it.

Our firm has dealt with cases in which a problem existed but no one took the steps necessary to rectify it or warn others about the potential problem, and the result spelled disaster for someone. It's in this process that we've been frequently able to identify the party or parties responsible for such oversights or negligence.

> We've been frequently able to identify the party or parties responsible for such oversights or negligence.

When the immediate needs of a personal injury victim have been taken care of, when the immediate turmoil in a victim's life is ebbing, the question will ultimately come, "What now?" The idea of a lawsuit might be the furthest thing from the mind of a victim and his or her family, but they owe it to themselves to at least look into the possibility that the accident victim might be entitled to compensation. This can include lost current and future wages, medical bills, pain and suffering, and other justifiable claims.

Someone who has been in an auto accident or suffered an injury at a store, for instance, can reasonably expect the other party's insurance to pay. If, however, someone suffers from another's intentional act such as an assault or a robbery, insurance most likely won't come into play; a lawsuit might be the only way to recover damages, and a personal injury lawyer's assistance can be invaluable on a number of levels.

## A Few "Don'ts"

Don't ever admit fault to paramedics, employers, investigators, or anyone else for that matter—even if they are close friends or family. Remember the line from so many cop shows, "Anything you say can and will be used against you." It's particularly true in personal injury cases; insurance companies will be quick to pounce on anything that can help them reduce or even eliminate the need for a payout.

The fact is, you should not talk to anyone about your case except your lawyer. Your conversations with your attorney are protected by the attorney-client privilege, but you could be giving up some of your rights in this area if you mention to others what you have discussed with your attorney. Don't get into conversations with claims adjusters or lawyers from even your own insurance company; keep in mind that it's chief goal is to limit the amount it pays out, not to help you.

> Don't get into conversations with claims adjusters or lawyers from even your own insurance company.

When it comes down to it, you most likely don't know all the factors that went into the accident you suffered. It could have been due to someone else's use of the tool or piece of machinery, or faulty maintenance you weren't aware of, a blown tire, and so on. The reality is that you simply can't know at the time if you were at fault at all. Things can happen way too quickly in an accident, and you just can't expect yourself to have all the facts of your injury at your fingertips. That's where a thorough investigation comes into play. This isn't a matter of lying or skirting the truth—it's simply a matter of understanding that in the heat of the moment you cannot expect yourself to know all the elements that could have contributed to your accident.

Even if it turns out that someone's actions contributed to an accident, he or she might not be completely at fault; there could be "outside" factors that contributed to the accident such as lack of maintenance or warnings on a piece of machinery, unsafe working conditions, someone else's mistake, and so on. You'll need expert and objective advice on this matter, and that can take place only after a thorough investigation has been completed. We've had plenty of experience at digging in to accidents and uncovering factors that contributed to unsafe conditions that had put our clients at unnecessary and avoidable risk.

Our work with personal injury victims has taught us the importance of getting an expert investigation underway as soon as possible. We retain trained, professional investigators and experts who will dig into all the facts of your accident. What they find can have a tremendous impact on your case, and it can counter "expert" testimony from an employer, a tool manufacturer, the supplier of a product or service. Keep in mind that there will be plenty of others out there who will be trying to protect their own interests any way they can.

## Call Us

No matter the circumstances surrounding the accident, no matter what you've been told, and no matter what you may think about the accident—give us a call. The quicker we can start looking into your case, the better able we will be to help protect your rights. We realize the burdens that personal injuries can place on victims and their families, and the idea of filing a lawsuit can look like just another complicating factor, but personal injury victims don't have to go it alone.

It's been our experience that personal injury victims who seek and get professional advice can greatly reduce their feelings of helplessness, bewilderment, and confusion—and it can also increase their chances of getting the compensation they deserve.

> Give us a call. The quicker we can start looking into your case, the better able we will be to help protect your rights.

# 2

# MIKE LOMBARDI'S SIX-STEP PROCESS TO SETTLE YOUR CASE

LOMBARDI LAW FIRM CONSISTENTLY REDEFINES THE PERSONAL approach to helping those who have been injured in an automobile accident or other serious injury. Out time-tested and results-driven system approach to these types of cases will maximize your claim.

## Step 1: Initial Meeting

The first thing I'll do is hear you out; I'll want to learn all the facts of your case, and I'll listen to you.

The next thing I'll do is explain the whole process I'll go through to obtain a fair settlement. I'll be careful to explain the role I'll play in the process and answer any questions you have or that I've raised.

My next step will involve obtaining all the information I can about you, your injuries—personal or property—and the treatment you've undergone or will have to undergo. And this includes a look into the future. If, say, you injured your knee in an accident, that could mean that five, ten years down the road, you might need a knee replacement. You and I together will go over all the possibilities.

I'll also thoroughly review your insurance coverage and that of the other motorist so we'll end up with a clear picture of coverage, limits, and so on.

## Step 2: You're Now under My "Protective Care"

I'll handle all the issues and problems that come up, including talking with adjusters, doctors, therapists, etc. I'll ask you to send me any bills, letters, and such that come your way.

At that point, I'll want to make sure you concern yourself with getting better and getting your life back on track.

## Step 3: Information Gathering

You can leave the information-gathering to me. I'll get copies of photos, witness statements, police reports, and copies of all your medical records and bills. I'll document all your lost wages, and this will include overtime that you would have worked had it not been for your accident.

I'll give you a good idea of other information I'll need to handle your case. This includes expenses you've incurred—taxi rides to your doctors or therapists, the ibuprofen and other drugs you've bought over the counter, even how many Ace bandages you've gone through—all your out-of-pocket expenses. I know from my experience that those can add up.

I'll also be interested in hearing from you how your accident has affected your life. Were you unable to attend your children's soccer games? Did you have to forgo using tickets you had for a ball game or a play? Have you had to hire someone to clean the house or unclog the gutters, things you would have normally been able to handle?

## Step 4: Demand and Negotiation

I'm hard hitting when it comes to negotiations. I'll take all the above information I've collected from you and present it as a "package" to the insurance company. In it, I'll give the company all the facts and figures and document every penny you're entitled to under the law. I'll let the insurance company know exactly how your life has been affected by your accident.

The insurance company will end up knowing you and I are as serious as can be in our desire to get you the compensation you deserve.

## Step 5: Litigation

Litigation, of course, is our last resort. When the insurance company realizes you and I are willing and able to go to court, they'll sit up and take notice.

In the meantime, I'll use the threat of an impending court date as leverage in trying to obtain a great settlement offer. I'll use the time to get in touch with experts to support us before and in the course of any trial.

> When the insurance company realizes you and I are willing and able to go to court, they'll sit up and take notice.

## Step 6: Building Lifelong Personal Relationships

My work on your behalf won't stop once you receive your settlement check. My goal is to become your go-to lawyer for all your legal needs, and I'll be particularly honored if you refer your friends and family to me. I'll show them the same attention to detail and determination I will have shown you. That's how I practice law—I want to develop personal relationships with my clients.

And if for any reason I cannot handle your case or those of the folks you send my way, you can count on me to be upfront about that and turn to my network to find a lawyer who can.

# 3

# INJURED IN AN AUTOMOBILE ACCIDENT?

YOU CAN COLLECT FOR INJURIES YOU SUFFERED IN A CAR accident. What's critical initially, of course, is you and anyone else injured getting prompt medical treatment. Even if you don't think you're injured severely enough to warrant going to the hospital to get checked out, you perhaps should do so. Calling the police, collecting the names and addresses of witnesses, and contacting your insurance company are other steps that auto accidents call for. The advent of smartphones has made it so much easier for victims of accidents to take pictures of the damage done on the spot and even record what witnesses have to say as well as their names and phone numbers.

We understand that, once the dust settles, getting your car back into working condition so you can work may be a necessity, but talk to us before you take it into the shop. Your case may require some solid documentation of the extent of your car's damages, and that will mean getting plenty of photos to be able to prove the extent of damages later. We also recommend that you get photos of the bruises, cuts, and so on that you suffered, as these will fade over time.

# 4

# INJURED ON THE JOB?

IN MOST CASES, THOSE WHO SUFFER ON-THE-JOB INJURIES cannot sue their employers. The Workers Compensation Act was passed to take care of those who were injured at work and to protect their employers against lawsuits. Such workplace injuries are handled without any rulings about who was at fault.

Workers' Compensation can help you while you are disabled due to an accident or if you end up permanently disabled. It can cover medical bills and lost pay and compensate the survivors in case of death, but it won't cover punitive damages and pain and suffering as can personal injury lawsuits.

Exceptions to this general rule, however, do exist. Let's consider a case of someone injured in an accident caused by a faulty piece of equipment or product actually manufactured by his or her employer. The victim could possibly sue the employer as the maker of a defective product. Here again is where it's critical to seek the advice of an attorney who is working for you, not one whose main task it is to protect the employer or the insurance company.

> Seek the advice of an attorney who is working for you, not one whose main task it is to protect the employer or the insurance company.

# 5

# INJURED BY A THIRD PARTY?

ACCIDENTS CAUSED BY SOMEONE OTHER THAN AN EMPLOYER can be much different stories when it comes to on-the-job accidents. Think about an outside trucking company delivering material to your jobsite or gas company workers making the final connections of a gas line into your place of work; if they are responsible for your accident, they could be sued even though the accident happened at work.

As well, someone required to drive for work who's in a vehicle accident may be able to sue the responsible party, again even though it may have been technically an "on-the-job" accident.

You can recover lost wages and medical expenses, damages for scarring, for pain and suffering, loss of companionship, emotional distress, and loss of enjoyment of life in such a suit, whether your accident is caused by someone's negligence or a defective product.

Here again, our firm will delve into important details you may have overlooked and determine who's responsible for an accident. You'll need prompt and thorough investigation of the accident itself to uncover all its ins and outs, and you'll need someone on your side to look into any third-party involvement in the accident by heading up a thorough, professional, and prompt investigation, which includes getting statements from witnesses, photographs, and other information that could fade or disappear over time.

# 6

# INJURED BY A PRODUCT?

IF YOU'VE BEEN INJURED BY A TOOL OR AN APPLIANCE AT HOME or a piece of machinery or equipment at work, the particular product's design may have played a role in your accident. It's critical that the tool or equipment be set aside and not altered, fixed, or changed—or worse, thrown away. It could be evidence that plays a critical role in establishing who's at fault—whether totally or in part.

One important point: anyone injured by a product, a tool, or any other implement should *never* use it again or let anyone else use it. Make sure everyone knows about the possibly defective tool or equipment. If you use it, that could be considered evidence that you didn't really consider it dangerous or at fault for your injury.

# 7
# RESULTS OF PERSONAL INJURIES SHORT TERM

- debilitating pain
- inability to work/lack of income
- medical problems that require immediate treatment and follow-up care
- large immediate debt

# 8

# RESULTS OF PERSONAL INJURIES LONG TERM

- need for intensive and extensive ongoing medical procedures, including surgery, skin grafts, etc.

- possibility of chronic pain and the treatment required for that

- increased susceptibility to cancer, etc.

- need for rehabilitation services

- dealing with the physical, emotional, and social problems resulting from permanent disfigurement

- loss of future wages, raises, and possible promotions

- having to pay for all of the above

# 9

# FINDING AN ATTORNEY

When it comes to personal injuries, you need a specialist in this complex field of law, not a jack-of-all-trades. The lawyer who handled your real estate closing or the lawyer who wrote up your will has specialized legal skills that don't necessarily transfer over to personal injury cases. Keep in mind, however, that those lawyers may be able to steer you to a personal injury lawyer they know of or have worked with who have great reputations in personal injury matters.

If you're a victim of a personal injury, you simply need an attorney well versed in this particular area of the law. The time you spend finding a personal injury lawyer with whom you can develop trust and rapport is time well spent.

Ask friends, coworkers, and family—they will have your best interests at heart. Even if they don't know of a personal injury lawyer, they may be able to recommend a lawyer who could direct you to one.

> The time you spend finding a personal injury lawyer with whom you can develop trust and rapport is time well spent.

You can spend some time on the Web looking for lawyers' organizations and directories of lawyers. Keep in mind, however, that caution is necessary here—some are simply lists of lawyers who have paid a fee to be listed, not necessarily those who are well versed in personal injury.

Be cautious as well about relying on lawyers' ads in the Yellow Pages, on billboards, or in TV or radio commercials. That type of advertising might just be a reflection of the amount of money a lawyer has for advertising, not his or her experience or competence, and the Yellow Pages and the billboard companies aren't going to check on their credentials.

You need an attorney who is willing and able to take your case to trial if necessary, not a lawyer who is simply going to fish for a quick settlement. For this reason, it's best to interview several attorneys. Look primarily for attorneys whose primary practice is in the area of personal injury. You're looking for an attorney not only with confidence, experience, and knowledge, but also someone you can trust explicitly with all the facts of your case.

If you hire a huge firm, your case could be lost among many others or handled primarily by legal assistants. On the other hand, a small firm might not have the resources to handle your case if it will end up involving expert witnesses and large-scale investigations. There are elements that you might not know are important to your case.

# 10

# STATUTES OF LIMITATIONS AND OTHER DEADLINES

Statutes of limitations are those laws that dictate time limits for filing suits. They establish how much time a victim of a personal injury has to file a lawsuit after an accident or injury, and you can be sure that whomever you are suing—a manufacturer, an insurance company, and so on—will not cut you any slack if you file after a statute of limitations deadline.

This is where accurate information is critical. Don't ever guess about a statute of limitations or rely on what you've heard from any source other than a lawyer who knows the statutes of limitations that apply to your case. Because statutes of limitations can vary wildly from state to state, a relative in one state who says you have two years could be wrong; you could find out your state gives you just one year.

The same goes for an attorney in a different state; he or she is sure to know the statutes of limitations there but not in your state. In addition, statutes of limitations can vary based on whether the case involves minors. If your case involves a matter in another state, you can count on us to get the straight information from one of the knowledgeable attorneys we've worked with across the country.

Speed is important in these matters. We've unfortunately heard over the years from clients who've relied on wrong or out-of-date information and have discovered too late that the statute of limitations has run out or has only a few months to run—not enough time for us to adequately prepare a case. Their delay at times was due to lack of information or even the thought they were responsible for an accident so didn't think they had a case—until it was too late. Some thought that they were victims of bad luck or were initially reluctant to file a lawsuit out of fear or embarrassment. They hadn't realized that even though they could have been partially responsible for an accident, others could have shared in the blame and could have been called upon to answer for that.

Our advice to you is regardless of your initial thoughts on an accident, set aside your assumptions and get our legal advice. You have the right to seek and receive objective advice about your accident, and if you do so in a timely fashion, you may not have to forgo justice and compensation because of a technicality. We've been contacted too late at times, but we've never been contacted too early.

> Regardless of your initial thoughts on an accident, set aside your assumptions and get our legal advice.

Keep in mind that certain "civic" or governmental agencies, including states, cities, and townships have very strict deadlines when it comes to someone filing a claim for damages against them. If, say, you were injured in an accident with a city or township garbage truck, you might find that you are subject to its rules and regulations when it comes to filing a lawsuit against it, and the time limits can be considerably shorter than if you were suing an insurance company.

It's important to think about "statutes of limitations" in a broader sense. Your case may be subject to other deadlines you have to comply with, for instance, getting a signed doctor's report into an insurance company, and that's where we can help. You can count on us to be in touch with your medical professionals and to keep any and all of these deadlines in mind. All too often, those suffering from personal injuries, and even their families, can have so much on their minds that they can benefit greatly from professional help when it comes to handling such demands.

We will get the t's crossed and the i's dotted to make sure the opposing parties cannot take advantage of a passed deadline—and they will if they can. Insurance companies are not in business to hand out money; their task is to keep it. They aren't going to offer justice; you need a lawyer in your corner willing to fight for the justice you deserve, and a single missed deadline could spell disaster for you or your loved one's legitimate claim.

# 11

# WHAT'S MY CASE WORTH?

THIS IS THE BIG QUESTION, OF COURSE, AND PERHAPS THE most difficult to handle. You can certainly claim all the specific, documented losses you have suffered, including lost wages, medical expenses, insurance co-pays, out-of-pocket expenses, and others.

If your injuries have long-term implications and will affect you financially (keep you from earning as much as you used to), physically (if you won't be able to do all that you used to do), or emotionally (your scars or other disfigurements are going to affect your social life), the courts could take these into consideration.

Your liability in your accident will come into play when it comes to calculating what your case may be worth. If the courts determine that you were, say, 25 percent or 50 percent liable for your accident, your award could be reduced by that percentage— this is an area in which different states have varying laws.

The other party's total assets, above and beyond insurance limits, could come into play here as well, as can your preexisting conditions and legal "caps" on the amount of awards.

Truth is, there are so many variables and factors when it comes to determining the "value" of any case, but I have learned that what's critical is first, solid documentation of all the facts, evidence, and so on, and second, solid presentation of all this evidence in a crystal-clear way to opposing attorneys, insurance adjusters, judges, and juries. This is the way we've learned to increase settlements way above the initial amounts offered.

# 12

# COMPENSATION YOU MAY BE ABLE TO COLLECT

The damages a victim of a personal injury suit can claim are numerous:

- **Past and Future Lost Wages:** Personal injury victims can claim wages they lost while they were off work, and this includes overtime that they would have worked, vacation time, and personal time and sick time they would have accrued if they were still on the job. In addition, it could be that due to their injuries, they're unable to earn the same amount they were earning before or have to forgo a promotion to a higher-paying job. These are the details we'll take into consideration when it comes to determining the total economic impact an accident causes.

- **Past and Future Medical Expenses:** Victims of personal injuries can require, in addition to immediate medical care—and that can be extensive and expensive—medical care that might be required even years later as a direct result of the injury. We're familiar with the necessity of getting expert medical advice to determine the likelihood of this.

- **Out-of-Pocket Expenses:** If you need to hire a housekeeper to take over tasks you used to manage yourself but can't because of your injuries, you can claim that in your case. The same goes for insurance co-payments and deductibles, medical equipment such as crutches, and so on. When in doubt, document it and save the receipts. We'll be able to offer you a list of all the out-of-pocket expenses you should document.

- **Past and Future Pain and Suffering:** When it comes to compensation for "pain and suffering," courts will consider not only the initial, immediate pain and suffering a personal injury victim has gone through but also the likelihood of long-term pain and suffering. Someone might end up with acute, chronic pain when it comes to using arms or legs.

- **Loss of Consortium:** "Loss of consortium" is a specific legal term that refers to the loss suffered by the spouse of a personal injury victim, who can have a legitimate claim to damages in this matter. He or she could suffer if the victim is unable to have sex, to offer the companionship (think here about a husband and wife no longer able to go camping, play tennis together, take walks around the block, or other activities they were accustomed to). Perhaps the injured party can no longer take care of the children or pitch in on household chores—the little and big things that make up marriage. Courts have long recognized that personal injuries can affect more than one person and can award damages based on this. This can get very personal, intimate, and potentially embarrassing. However, this is an area in which you'll be able to rely on our professionalism, tact, compassion, and willingness to listen to you.

- **Enjoyment of Life:** Nobody can calculate the correct dollar amount for something as broad and subjective as "enjoyment of life." How can anyone put a price tag on not being able to shoot hoops with a son or teach a daughter to swim? However, the courts do consider such losses as real damages, and they'll consider them when making awards.

- **Emotional Distress:** Personal injury victims who end up with permanent disfigurements such as scars, burns, or missing limbs can suffer ongoing emotional distress as they worry about the present and also realize they could be affected socially for a long time, perhaps even for the rest of their lives.

- **Damaged Property:** This can include damages to your car or home or compensation for stolen items.

- **Punitive Damages:** Courts have awarded punitive damages to victims of personal injury; they're meant to punish the guilty party for his or her actions beyond what the court deems the victim should receive for his or her losses.

> Punitive damages are meant to punish the guilty party for his or her actions beyond what the court deems the victim should receive for his or her losses.

# 13

# DISABILITY CLAIMS

DISABILITY CLAIMS ARE ANOTHER AREA IN WHICH WE'VE BEEN able to help many clients. At times, insurance companies that offer individual disability policies and ERISA policies (one of the benefits some employers offer their employees) can drag their feet or even deny the benefits personal injury victims deserve. If this is your case, you can rely on us to handle the matter. Our firm has the experience and the aggressive attitude needed to make sure our clients receive what they are due, whether these are short-term or long-term disability claims.

I know from a lot of experience with disability benefits that they can be—make that are—very detailed contracts that anyone not in that business can really struggle to understand. Our law offices have regularly done battle with these insurance companies and their complex jargon; we have the resources you need to help you wherever you are in the country.

# 14

# POST-ACCIDENT: THE NEXT STEPS

IT'S TOUGH FOR VICTIMS OF PERSONAL INJURIES, EVEN AFTER they get out of the hospital and perhaps back to work to think much beyond the immediate: How am I going to shop? Can I still pick up the kids? What about my last three missed paychecks? It's tough at times like these for personal injury victims to even contemplate the future.

Though determining what the future holds may be too much for you to take in all at once, consider taking some short but concrete steps one at a time on behalf of yourself and your loved ones.

- Contact our office before you respond to any requests for information from insurance adjusters, investigators—anyone—and never sign anything until we've had a chance to review it.

- Save all the information that comes your way—records, emails, notes, letters, statements and so on from doctors, hospitals, the ambulance company, etc. We'll need these, and you don't want to rely on someone to resend a document by the time you might need it. Make copies of everything, or ask our office to do so. Even if organization is not your strong suit, the ante here is upped, and this is an area where you can make a difference by helping us protect your rights.

- Keep accurate records of all the time you have missed from work or had to take off because of doctors' appointments.

- Keep a journal of your medical, physical complications—aches, pains, anxiety, and dates, times, and places.

- Keep all your medical appointments, and follow your doctors' and physical therapists' advice to the T—failure to do so could make it look as though your injuries weren't as serious as they really were.

- If you ever need help in any of these matters, don't be shy or embarrassed—ask our office for help. We have or can put you in touch with all the resources you'll need.

# 15

# STEPS WE'LL TAKE IN HANDLING YOUR CASE

PERSONAL INJURY CASES CAN BECOME UNDERSTANDABLY overwhelming for anyone not that knowledgeable about the laws involved and how they might apply to his or her case. We're used to mastering lengthy and complicated checklists of tasks and details that will start with our initial consultation and go all the way to the courtroom if necessary.

This is just to say that you need a professional in your corner at all times during what can be a long process. We pride ourselves on working for our clients one step at a time, staying ahead of the curve, and keeping them informed as their cases proceed.

This is just a brief rundown on what you can expect from us.

- an initial consultation in which we'll listen to all the particulars of your case and ask questions
- a fair, unbiased opinion as to the merits of your case and the likelihood of your winning
- contacting doctors and collecting all relevant medical information, including hospital records and bills
- undertaking a thorough, expert investigation of the accident scene and any equipment or tools involved

- interviewing witnesses
- filing motions
- handling depositions
- advising you on the fairness of settlement offers considering your needs, current and future (An attorney experienced in dealing with insurance companies' claims adjusters are generally able to negotiate settlements way above what the victim would be able to negotiate on his or her own.)
- filing a lawsuit
- letting you know what will be involved in arbitration
- handling the "discovery" process—reviewing the other side's story and evidence prior to any trial
- preparing you, all witnesses, and any relevant evidence for trial
- going to trial with confidence

# 16

# PAYING FOR LEGAL REPRESENTATION

LOMBARDI LAW FIRM STICKS BEHIND ITS "NO FEE GUARANTEE." This means that if we don't recover on your behalf, there's no legal fee. I'll make sure that you have a complete, thorough understanding of all the financial details, and I'll put them in writing.

> If we don't recover on your behalf, there's no legal fee.

# 17

# CONTACT ME

I HOPE THIS BOOK HAS HELPED YOU AS YOU CONSIDER YOUR situation as a victim or a loved one of a personal injury, particularly automobile accidents. I also hope I've sufficiently stressed the complexity of personal injury cases and the absolute need of your retaining a lawyer who is knowledgeable, experienced, and diligent in pursuing your case.

The fact that I can't stress enough is that insurance companies are in the business of doling out less money than they take in—not offering you a fair, just settlement. They continually try to lowball claims and argue that what you'll spend on a lawyer will exceed what you can expect as a settlement. Don't believe them.

We're used to these tactics; we know how the insurance industry operates, the tricks it can try to pull on unsuspecting claimants, and their reliance on people not knowing the law. We're able to spot lowball offers based on our broad experience in the field of personal injury, and we're willing to engage in tough negotiations and go to court with the tenacity necessary to get you the results—and the justice—you deserve.

# CONCLUSION

RESULTS MATTER IN ALL LEGAL MATTERS, AND THEY'RE particularly important in personal injury cases. The outcome will affect you and your loved ones today and for years to come. There's no reason you should have to forgo your dreams of college for your children, weddings, vacations, and a comfortable retirement because of the actions of others.

Of course, no attorney can guarantee the outcome of your case. That disclaimer on investment literature that reads, "Past results are no guarantee of future performance" is there for a good reason.

Nonetheless, I want to stress the fact that I have handled literally thousands of auto accident cases, and I have a tremendous success rate when it comes to obtaining the settlements my clients have justly deserved. My firm is one that not only the courts but also the insurance companies and their attorneys have come to respect.

**Mike Lombardi & Associates**
**Injury and Accident Lawyers**
1011 Smith Street
Providence, RI 02908
Phone: 401 751 6100
Email: ml@lombardirusso.com
Website: www.lombardilawoffice.com

# ABOUT THE AUTHOR

MICHAEL LOMBARDI IS A NATIVE RHODE ISLANDER, HAVING been born in Johnston. He attended Johnston High School and excelled academically and athletically. He was a four-year starter on the football team and received awards for making the statewide all-academic team. He attributes that to the values his coach instilled in him; his coach had been influenced by legendary coach Vince Lombardi (no relation) and the values he stressed of teamwork, commitment, hard work, sacrifice, the will to win, excellence, passion, and results. Michael's coach repeatedly told him, "If you subscribe to these principles on the field, you must also subscribe to them in life," and Michael has done just that.

He graduated from Johnston High in 1997 and from Rhode Island College in 2002 with a bachelor's in political science. He attended Roger Williams Law School in Bristol, Rhode Island. Throughout his years in school, he worked part-time as a valet at top restaurants. People would see him bundled up outside in 20-degree weather eating a bowl of soup and studying in between hustling to retrieve cars. He learned a lot from the service industry and interacted with people from all walks of life. Long and disciplined days were his trademark from early on.

After graduating from law school, he went to work for a law firm in Providence, where he focused on personal injury and criminal law for ten years. He was an innovator, motivator, and legal strategist who dreamed of opening his own firm.

In 2015, he did just that. He wanted his firm to operate on the core principles he had learned at a young age. He has taken Vince Lombardi's advice to heart: "The achievements of an organization are the results of the combined efforts of each individual ... People who work together will win together whether it be against complex defenses or problems of modern society." Michael's objective was to play fairly, decently, by the rules—and win.

Today, he applies his energy, discipline, and will to win to serving and satisfying his clients. He'll strategize with his team to ensure you get the best possible outcome whether it's getting the most money out of a settlement or taking it to trial if necessary.

His rigid adherence to his six-step process (see chapter 2) ensures that his clients receive as much money as possible as quickly as possible.

Out of the office, you'll find Michael cooking, watching the New England Patriots, traveling, and spending time with his wife, son, and French bulldog Zoey.

## A Case in Point—Don't Sign! The Delayed-Treatment Trick

One of my clients was in a car accident. Besides the damage to his car, he was suffering from a sore back and a very stiff neck. My concern was that the accident had happened about thirty days earlier. An insurance adjuster had made an offer to settle the case and handle his medical bills but didn't tell him that he should seek follow-up treatment if necessary. My client, who was confused as to what to do, didn't accept the offer, but he took about a month before he saw me. He was still in pain, but the insurance company tried to use that four-week gap in treatment against him to reduce the amount it would have to pay on his claim; it said that my client's delay was an indication that his injuries weren't that severe. In this case, however, their quick offer and the false sense of caring for the victim had caused the delay in the first place. Fortunately, we were able to negotiate a fair settlement for the client. The moral of the story is call a lawyer as quickly as you can!

## A Case in Point—A Low-Ball Offer after Treatment

A client who had been involved in an auto accident hadn't immediately sought my advice. Within hours of the accident, an insurance adjuster had called her and in a very calm, pleasant voice said that his company really cared about her situation and said there was no need for her to call a lawyer. She saw a chiropractor for about a month after the accident, thinking everything would turn out okay. During the treatment, the insurance company pressured her to settle, but she became suspicious because the offer was low and she was still in pain. She wondered if it would be enough to see her through the care she needed. She was right to wonder about that. We took over the case and got a settlement three times the initial offer.

## A Case in Point—The Importance of Timely and Expert Investigation

I had a client tell me he'd fallen off a ten-foot deck that was in poor condition. We immediately sent out investigators, including a construction expert, to look at the deck. We obtained an opinion from the expert and took plenty of photos of the deck. The insurance company accepted full responsibility for my client's damages due in large part to the quick and thorough investigation we had conducted. If we had delayed, the insurance company would have argued that the deck had been safe at the time of the accident.

## A Case in Point—Auto Accident and Obtaining Video

Jim came into my office after being rear-ended. The other driver had come up with a seemingly convincing story that Jim had backed into him. We hustled and got hold of a video that had been taken across the street that clearly showed my client being rear-ended. The insurance company immediately changed its position and paid Jim's claim. Our swift action made a huge difference in the outcome of his case; without it, the insurance company would have denied the claim based on what its driver had said.

## A Case in Point—Don't Sign: The Property Damage Trick

Robert came into my office and told me about the injuries he had sustained in a car accident. He had in hand a check from the insurance company that it said would cover the damages to his car. He was complimentary about that; he said an agent had actually come out to his house to inspect the car and had given him the check on the spot. I told him he should seek the advice of an expert on auto body repairs to determine if there was more, particularly hidden, damages to the car. Robert did, and he got a lot more money.

Insurance companies love it when people cash those low-ball checks because they'll turn around and say, "How could you have sustained significant physical harm when it took only $1,000 to fix your car?"

This is why my firm, unlike many others, will help you settle the property damage part of your case at absolutely no charge!

## A Case in Point—Don't Sign: The Medical Bill Trick

Brenda settled her case without a lawyer. She came to me with the settlement check and a stack of medical bills. She was confused about what medical bills she had to pay and how much she had to pay. The adjuster hadn't told her she might have to pay the medical bills in full. She wasn't aware she had the right to negotiate down her medical bills and keep the difference. Fortunately, we were able to handle the whole matter for her and save her a lot of money.

# APPENDIX

## ACCIDENT CASES IN MASSACHUSETTS AND RHODE ISLAND—SOME BIG DIFFERENCES

IT'S IMPORTANT FOR ME TO MAKE SURE MY READERS understand some important differences between accident cases in Massachusetts and Rhode Island. There are certainly many commonalities, but there are a number of very important differences as well.

First, Massachusetts is considered a no-fault insurance state; this means that regardless of fault, your own insurance company will pay your medical bills. Under this no-fault system, your medical bills could be paid from a number of sources including:

- **Personal Injury Protection (PIP):** This is additional auto insurance that will pay a minimum of $2,000 and a maximum of $8,000 for medical bills and lost wages.

- **MedPay:** This is optional medical coverage offered to drivers and occupants for reasonable medical expenses for necessary medical treatment. This optional coverage kicks in when PIP benefits are exhausted

- **Private Health Insurance**

- **Medicare or Medicaid**

- **Workers Compensation**

Under this no-fault system, compensation owed to an accident victim by a third party could be reduced by the amount the victim's PIP policy paid him or her.

Keep in mind that PIP insurance won't compensate you for pain and suffering. Under Massachusetts no-fault law, you can bring a claim or sue the person who caused the accident for pain and suffering only if one of the following conditions is met.

- medical bills total more than $2,000

- you have suffered serious injury such as a broken bone, a disfiguring scar, a permanent eye injury, or permanent hearing damage

On the other hand, Rhode Island law doesn't require PIP and doesn't have a threshold requirement that must be met before an auto accident victim can bring a claim or sue for pain and suffering.

It can become very complex to determine how all these potential payers—PIP, MedPay, your private health insurance, Medicare, Medicaid, Workers Comp—will view your specific case and determine what they have to pay. This is an excellent reason you need a qualified and knowledgeable attorney on your side.

## Fault—Determined Differently in Massachusetts and Rhode Island

Massachusetts is what's known as a "modified comparative fault" state, and this can have a big impact on your case and the settlement. In a nutshell, if it's determined that you are more than 50 percent at fault for your accident, you cannot receive any compensation from the other driver for your pain and suffering. This could be the case in an accident in which you were T-boned at an intersection by someone driving at a high rate of speed but you were making an illegal right-hand turn at the time.

On the other hand, you might be found to be only 20 percent responsible for the accident. That would mean you might be awarded $100,000, but that would be reduced by 20 percent.

On the other hand, Rhode Island is a pure comparative fault state. That means that a plaintiff could recover 1 percent even if he or she was found to be 99 at fault. In Rhode Island, it's easier to bring a claim or suit if you're found to be mostly at fault for the accident.

The takeaway here is that you should never rely on what you hear on the streets, so to speak. It could be well intentioned but just plain wrong information that could have a disastrous effect on your case. Give me a call!

**MIKE LOMBARDI & ASSOCIATES**

**INJURY AND ACCIDENT LAWYERS**

1011 SMITH STREET

PROVIDENCE, RI 02908

PHONE: 401 751 6100

EMAIL: ML@LOMBARDIRUSSO.COM

WEBSITE: WWW.LOMBARDILAWOFFICE.COM

WA